MY DARLING FROM THE LIONS

Published by Tin House, Portland, Oregon

Distributed by W. W. Norton & Company

Library of Congress Cataloging-in-Publication Data

Names: Long, Rachel, 1988– author.
Title: My darling from the lions / Rachel Long.
Description: Portland, Oregon : Tin House, [2021]
Identifiers: LCCN 2021019391 | ISBN 9781951142711 (paperback) |
    ISBN 9781951142797 (ebook)
Subjects: LCGFT: Poetry.
Classification: LCC PR6112.O5259 M93 2021 | DDC 821/.92—dc23
LC record available at https://lccn.loc.gov/2021019391

First US Edition 2021
Printed in the USA
Interior design by Jakob Vala

www.tinhouse.com

MY DARLING FROM THE LIONS

RACHEL LONG

 TIN HOUSE / Portland, Oregon

CONTENTS

OPEN

Open · 3

Hotel Art, Barcelona · 4

Night Vigil · 6

Sandwiches · 7

The Clean · 8

Open · 10

Bike · 11

8 · 14

Open · 16

Apples · 17

Helena · 19

The Garden · 21

Open · 23

Portent · 24

The Yearner · 25

Red Hoover · 26

Open · 29

A LINEAGE OF WIGS

Orb · 33

Referring to the House as the Whole Street · 34

The Musical Box · 35

So Low · 37

Mum's Snake · 38

The Cow and the Moon · 42

Car Sweetness · 43

Bloodlines · 44

And then there was the time I got into a fight · 45

Jail Letter · 46

Wire · 47

Red Roof · 48

Danielle's Dad · 50

Inside · 52

Divine Healing · 53

Night · 55

Communion · 57

Funeral Brochure · 60

Holiday Album · 61

The Omen · 62

DOLLS

Interview with B. Tape II · 65

Steve · 68

Black Princess! Black Princess! · 69

Self-Portrait with Baby · 71

Thanksgiving · 73

Other Women's Babies · 74

Acknowledgements · 77

OPEN

OPEN

This morning he told me
I sleep with my mouth open
and my hands in my hair.
I say, *What, like screaming?*
He says, *No, like abandon.*

HOTEL ART, BARCELONA

We're eating roses on a rooftop. The Med beneath us.
They serve clouds here too, I say.
Light starter? Wink.

Are they fluffy or black?
The waiter doesn't answer.

Every table is white except ours.
We sit at a naked woodblock. Antique;
There's enough of an age gap here,
need they have added 200 years?

The razor clams arrive in straight lines.
What's the matter?

We discuss kids. Maybe it's the wine,
or because my belly is beginning to push
against the bones of my dress. You say,
I don't think I'll identify with a brown son.

Excuse me, I stand,
spill your sparkling water.
You only notice your steak.

Contorting myself three ways in the toilet mirror,
I decide I won't look like this forever.
I don't even look like this now.

Dessert is air from a porcelain pump.
What if he has your eyes? I dare,
after another glass.

Back in our borrowed bathroom, I throw up rose foam,
a blade of grass. Who says *he* isn't a daughter?

I join you on the balcony. You hold me from behind,
lean us over, count . . .
We're as many storeys up as our age gap.

Why do you always have to—
Shhh. You lift my dress. I shoulder-width my legs,
is love not this?—gripping a fence in the sky.

NIGHT VIGIL

I was a choir-girl. Real angel
—lightning-faced and giant for my age.

Mum let us stay up late
if we went with her to night vigil.

It started at midnight, a time too exciting to fathom.
How the minute and the hour stood to attention!

During Three Members' Prayer, my sister fell asleep
under a chair, so she never knew

how I sang. Or how I fell silent
when the evangelist with smiling eyes said in his pulpit voice,

Here, child.
Had she woken, I would have told her, *Sleep, sleep!*

so she'd never know Smiling Eyes
also meant teeth,

or that he had blown candles for hands,
with which he led me down an incensed corridor,

and I followed.

SANDWICHES

Tiff's got me against the school railings, doing
my eyeliner. In double French, I'd whispered,
Your eyes. Will you make mine like that?—slice
through a room, a lie, a man—*Break time*
her body on mine, stoosh then soft; sugar
on the tongue of all she hasn't done yet, all she's
heard she could do. Already, Tiff's a reckoning;
bomb glitter on lids, oil spill on lips, sandwiches
padding her bra. Yeah, the sandwiches.
Thick, white, unbuttered. See, Tiff's clocked
the boys have clocked the difference between
a tissue and a tit, a sock and a tit, but not quite yet
a tit and a slice of bread. O, girl, you have opened
my eyes, how they weep!

THE CLEAN

white bowl of it.
The pile of it. Imagine
eating all the snow
you've ever wanted
in one sitting,
not having to pay for it.
The avocado of it.
Toast butter
cascading your fingers,
pink prosecco.
You'd be spaced-out,
clucking, grumpy,
sexless, you'd die
without this,
clutching your ribs
in the dark,
one street from home,
footsteps gathering—
I know a place
that is snow falling
from the Artex ceiling
into a room
you will never return to.
A promise
piling like cable knit.
4-ply snow-day snow.

I know a place where
the sad can't go,
where it'll never have
the right footwear.
Here, you can throw it all in.
Go on, baby, give it back
to whence it came.
Dispel three dinosaur dinners
like forgiveness,
like it never happened.
Bile is the bottom.
Ground zero.
There is no more after,
no more.
Girl, you can be new,
surrender it all
into one bowl. This,
your hollow.

OPEN

This morning, she told me
I sleep with my mouth open
and my hands in my hair.
I say, *What, Tiff, like screaming?*
She says, *No, Rach, like abandon.*

BIKE

Tyres fast over gravel
sounds like pissing

Something tells her
not to go as far
as the abattoir

The sign for Deer ½ mile
has collapsed
by the roadside

She calls him deer
for his stubborn gentleness,
his legs in the tan dress
that hasn't suited her for years

There! Through those trees
her teenage bedroom
in the upstairs window
of someone else's house

Sometimes she looks down
at her feet now and asks,
who the hell do you think you are?

—trainers flecked with grass,
cycling through the countryside, a shock
of yellow headscarf

He, too, calls her deer
but she can't be, can she?

—What doe would've worn fishnets
to a house party of hunters,
taken a pissy lift up
to their fifteenth-floor cabin
and knocked?

Run!
In these hooves?
Through an estate
built like Tetris?

Have you ever fled uphill—
hill of concrete,
acres of balconies identical
unanswerable doors—
reciting Psalm 23?

She speeds downhill
takes her feet off the pedals
surely goodness and mercy will follow me

Her bike wobbles
a tooth loose
in the mouth of the road

Deer have milk teeth
They lose them
at eighteen months old.

8

'Purge me with hyssop, and I shall be clean: wash me, and I shall be whiter than snow.'

—Psalm 51:7

this memory can't skip   it hops
on one leg   the other   making
the buckles on my mary janes
bounce then clang   cute shackles   my feet
will hopscotch-land on 8   *wash me*
at 8 i can't tell time   i'm led
through school and play   tea then bed at
8   i can't read faces   tell hands
to stop   unfreeze my grin   that room
his weight   *wash me and I shall be*
the girls at school call that place mini
but mum says it's a front bottom
i've a back bottom and if she
catches me with any other
dirty in my mouth she'll   *wash me*
and I shall be wash me wash   till
time decides itself   till i'm pressed
apple   against that wall   that sunday
that school   *wash wash   wash me*   over
his shoulder   there   on a tiny chair
the bible   just lying there   how
i have   and don't have   all birthdays

14

in this one   chalked moment   *wash me*
and I shall be whiter than   touched
by the hand of his clock i am
instantly older   *wash me   I*
wash me   I shall be whiter   than
it all speeds up   hopscotch in heels
eyes wide   coked up   *wash me I wash*
me I whiter than   gloss slathering
the hole that is my mouth or my
cunt   *purge me with hyssop and I*
shall be   I shall be   wash   because
i know its proper name   now   yes
mum   its proper place   for men to
crawl out and in   out and   *purge me*
with hyssop and I shall be I
shall be I shall be I shall be
snow

OPEN

This morning she told me
I sleep with my mouth open
and my hands in my hair.
I say, *What, Mum, like screaming?*
She says, *No, baby, like abandon.*

APPLES

Last night, I missed my train by seconds.
So close that one part of me did catch it
and waved from the window to the other half
still panting on the platform, tits play-doughing
out of a shit bra. I couldn't sleep for an hour
and a quarter—the exact time between the two
slices of me reaching home, in separate taxis,
each driven by a brother who co-owned the firm.
Today, I'm assuming the recovery position
in my favourite outfit—a jumper with no knickers,
the perfect hot/cold combo,
like a bowl of baked crumble and ice cream.
I am magazine educated, so have known for a while
that my body is an apple. Supporting theory:
I bruise so easy I worry it's leukaemia.
No, the doctor says, again, *it's just your dark skin.*
She recommends scar serum.

When I was bored after service—Mum still counting
the collection then insisting on sweeping from altar to street—
I'd sit in front of a pillar, playing with my brain-Barbie.
She was brown with tattoos and I made her have sex
with a grown man in a toilet cubicle.
I don't remember her face, or her body.
Nor what I named her. Something beginning with N . . .
When the mum of my then-best friend said

her daughter wasn't allowed to play with me
because I was another N-word—meaning
Mum went round in her dressing-gown to slap her silly
with her tongue, then returned to scatter the kitchen
and shred Dad's *Guardian* for not sticking up for us,
for never saying anything—

After that I had a sleep-dream
in which I grew a bright green face;
granny-smith hued, high polished.
And even though I was green,
I was The Most Beautiful Woman in the World.
I had the best hair
and even did humanitarian work.
I was interviewed
about both things,
each night, for TV.

HELENA

So the club's closing any minute, I'd made a bit but was dead
  on my feet. Then this old fucker comes in wanting a private
dance. He was the spit of my dad. Swear down. One point I had
  to tell him to sit on his hands. Gross init. But I weren't about to
say no to 300 quid. Fucking hell, all they bang on about is their
  wives, daughters or bank accounts, while I'm there tits-out.
You know Ali? I shake my head. Tiff says, who the bouncer?
  Yeah, the bouncer, lanky cunt. He waited for me to finish, grab
my shit from the dressing room, then asks if I want a lift. I'm like,
  yeah, alright, cos Crackhead Christina was s'posed to drive tonight
but she got drunk with some Simon Cowell lookalike, never even
  made that much out of him, idiot. Anyway, lanky Ali is like, babes,
no worries, where can I drop you? Next thing I know he's like,
  I just need to pick something up from my boy's, gimme two
minutes. Ten minutes later now he comes out the flats to say his
  boy's on his way, do I wanna come in and wait? I was like,
Ali, mate, I'm not being funny, I'm tired, I wanna go home.
  He's like, babe, I know, I hear you. Then just opens the fucking
passenger door. So, I go up to this grot-hole, curl up on the sofa.
  Next thing I know, this prick's kissing my neck, hand between
my legs. I'm like, Ali, what are you doing? I will piss on you,
  fucker! But maybe cos I was tired or whatever, I dunno but it felt
alright. He took my heels off, rubbed my feet and that—even
  sucked my big toe. I was like, stop, that's weird. He was like,
well, what else can I put in my mouth? Tiff and I grab each
  other's nighties. I know, right? I was like, what are you, a dog?

He was like, I can be. We all squeal. Who says that? So fucking
   cheesy! Then, he unzips my jeans. So, I'm like, fine, he can lick
me out, but I want it just like a bedtime story. So he's down there
   for like two seconds, then just stands up to take his jeans off.
I'm like, No, Ali! What are you doing? Kept saying No, Ali,
   what the fuck, Ali! Didn't care, I swear, as soon as his dick was
out he turned into a monster. Flipped me over, started acting out
   some horror-porn shit, pressing my head down like it was a fucking
apple into that rancid sofa. It reeked! God, like actual dog shit. Then
   he ripped my legs apart and started spitting into my vagina. Like,
actually gobbing inside of me. Oh my God! My God, I'm so
   angry. Helena sets her box of wings down, places her head between
her knees, starts screaming. Tiff doesn't tell her to stop. I don't either.
   Helena's screaming meets Scarlett's. They have a bit of a competition
till Helena starts laughing, hysterical like, I need to use your shower.
   Tiff nods, goes to lift Scarlett out her cot. Helena laughs herself down
and off the sofa, blonde hair dragging across the black pleather.
   She saunters to the bathroom. Before slamming the door, shouts
over her shoulder, *I promise I won't stay in it forever.*

THE GARDEN

Dinner was leftovers
followed by silence.
Days later you're still sat, staring ahead
in your blossoming wrap dress.

If the rose at your breast grows any larger
you're going to have to say something.
Darling, I'm late. Or: *You shit,*
I'm a garden with a rake in it.

Calm down. Wait. Watch
the one at your stomach dilate.
Throw up in the kitchen sink.
Return to your seat.

You can't give a man like him
news like this
and not have a portion of chips
steaming at the centre of it.

Choose the basement or the bedroom.
Go, now. Fasten the black veil
though no woman has shown you how.
Kneel at the lit throat of a candle.

Beg forgiveness for the thing you haven't done yet.
Say the prayer to rid you of bloom.
Say it in the tongue your mother might've taught you.
Who will you be this time around?

—Will you allow a flower to open
like a door from your mouth,
or does a bouquet of horsewhips
bloom from your right hand?

OPEN

This afternoon he told me
I dozed with my mouth open
and my arm over my eyes.
I say, *What, like hiding?*
He says, *No, like before a surprise.*

PORTENT

I feel middle class when I'm in love.
I think it's all the poached eggs on bird-seed bread,
staying up all night on Zoopla—imagine
waking under cottage beams,
the laughter in a garden. Kids.
A little boy with gold hair
keeps standing in my dreams.

I read somewhere that it takes three hundred years,
about thirteen generations, to change your social class.
I think about this whilst having a fag-I'm-quitting,
head against the doorbell—it's broken
but sometimes, after My Love has left for work,
after his hand-held shower, and a pee
in the gaffer-taped loo, I hear it
ringing and ringing.

THE YEARNER

I stacked three pillows, made sure
my head was heavy with bills, wine, yesterday's
deadline, and I slept hard, tight
as cement on my left arm. The needles came.
At dawn, I dragged it
like a salmon from under my body.
A part of me is dead. Now
I can shake my own hand,
meet myself again for the first time.
How my fingers feel to one another, strangers,
for a tingling moment, I am another.
Promise? This time will be different.

RED HOOVER

He was ridiculously good-looking. He was even Nigerian
—though Mum flits between this being a good thing in people
and the worst. I pulled his photo up on the internet, showed her.
She decided, on the spot, his Nigerianness was a good thing.
It was easy to pull his photo up on the internet
because he was an actor. I'd met him in a theatre.
He'd just been awarded a £3000 cheque
for being a Nigerian actor. It was a very hot summer.
I wore a black playsuit belonging to my younger sister
but carried a blazer—for a look that said: serious play.
He offered to buy me a drink. Of course
I said I'd prefer to buy my own, and when he insisted
I said OK like it was quite inconvenient for me to agree.
When our drinks were on the bar and glistening
in the velvet heat, he handed the barman his cheque.
Ha ha ha, said the barman. Ha ha ha, I said.
So, the ridiculously good-looking Nigerian had jokes.

On my lunchbreak, I found a clean bench to call him from.
We were awkward. I wanted him to ask me out.
Why wasn't he asking me out? Mum began asking after him,
where's that good-looking Nigerian? Don't tell me
you've ruined it already.

The second time, I spread out on my bed,
swung my legs up the wall—cold and good for my nerves.
It was a short call because someone was knocking at his door.
OK, I said like it was of no inconvenience whatsoever.
I slid my legs back down the wall.

A week later, I was standing in his living room
wearing my coat, or it was over my arm, my shoes still on.
Either we were just about to go out, or I'd just arrived
and he hadn't yet said, *Here, let me take your coat*
or, *Please, take off your shoes.*
He was running all over the house.
Upstairs then down, zooming around.
He was running a bath, then letting the water out
only to fill it back up. He ducked into a cupboard
and yanked a hoover. A red hoover.
He began hoovering everywhere,
he even hoovered the ceiling.
He just walked up the wall
and as he did, looked over his shoulder,
at me on the floor and said,
this won't take long, I just have to—

When I told Mum, she shook her head, laughed,
half lemon, half sugar. He's crazy, she shrugged.
God's showing you it won't work out
because he's all over the place. Shame. That good-looking man . . .
Nigerians, she sighed, always into something.

I'd still look him up on the internet sometimes.
Just to keep up to date with his plays, the BBC dramas.
Then I stopped. For years I didn't think of him.
OK, perhaps, but in a loose and smirking way;
playful, no serious pining. What was there to pine really?
Then, in bed one night, watching an adaptation
on my laptop, the ridiculously good-looking Nigerian
walks across the screen. His name escapes my mouth;
half sigh, half whistle. I say it like damn. I say it like,
man, where have you been? He has a few lines
then he's stabbed on a street I recognise
having danced down a long time ago.
Long before I met him at that theatre,
with his cheque folded into his pocket.
I remember our two awkward phone calls
and him hoovering his ceiling
and I laugh into my pillow
as he bleeds out.

OPEN

Tonight he told me
I fell asleep in the chair
with my head back,
my arms tight at my sides.
I say, *What, like bracing for impact?*
He says, *No, like working something out
with the sky.*

A LINEAGE OF WIGS

ORB

Mum combs her auburn 'fro up high.
So high it's an orb.
Everyone wants to—but cannot—touch it.

REFERRING TO THE HOUSE AS THE WHOLE STREET

Leywick Street is a three-storey, four-bedroom townhouse
in Stratford. Ten children live there. Top-and-tail.
They're all washed, fed and prayed for by a midwife

who, after another long nightshift, slips her shoes off
and pads into the kitchen, where she hangs her wig
over the ear of her chair,

and reaches for the sugared almonds
which come in various shades of dawn.
She holds each one up against the window

before popping it into her mouth
—pop—
and sighing.

THE MUSICAL BOX

Long before she's my Mum,
Ibi has a musical box.
When she opens it
with a tiny key, so tiny
one could swallow it,
a ballerina pops up
and begins pirouetting to music
like stars falling
onto four-poster beds.

Long before he's my big cousin,
David creeps into Ibi's room
while she's at school,
or at the fish market
before school.
He's heard the stars falling
from his room—the boy's room
down the corridor,
all heat and socks.

After being rattled and prised,
the box splays open.
The little ballerina, off-kilter,
begins dancing for her visitor.
She's pretty. Prettier
between his big fingers.

She feels like plasticine
so he squeezes.
The stars pause mid-air.

SO LOW

Mum lies on the sofa
like an arrowed queen
clutching her head
and low-groaning so low
only I can hear
from inside her.

MUM'S SNAKE

Firstly, Mum wouldn't like that I've called it her snake.
It wasn't my snake! It was the snake she put on me.

*

Every time Mum tells it she rubs the back of her hand
like a penny. She rubs the red-brown back of her hand.
I had to shave it down to this—not a hair, she says,
for years. She rubs the back of her hand.

*

Hair is a crowning glory.
A source not only of beauty but power.
Remember Samson?
It can be taken,
buried in the woods at night.
Everything you came into this world with,
all you were to achieve,
the love you were meant for,
trodden, rotting under the earth.
Don't let any of your aunties touch your hair at the party.
If one of them even reaches out for you, run,
come and find me.

*

Lord deliver me. My enemies wage war against me.

*

You don't have to believe me. It will take an incredible
leap of faith. My sister put a snake—a huge one, the kind
that swallows lambs, what's that sort called? A python, yeah,
or an anaconda maybe, but worse because it didn't belong to
this realm, wasn't of the physical, you see.
She put one of those on top of my head. I could feel it
moving. The migraines, my God, they were cosmic.
I couldn't stand the weight of it. I had to get it off,
I couldn't get it off. I was back and forth from the church,
sometimes three times a day—before work, after it,
once you were in bed. The elders tried everything.
The things I had to do, I cannot say.

*

Mum's American sister—the one whose name
will not be said in our house, the betrayal too great—
ecstatic. Dancing on a stage ecstatic.

*

At last, one old prophet from Nigeria heard about me,
said he'd seen something like this long ago.
He said let me speak to her. I spoke to him. God bless him.
He said, take clippers,
the snake is using your hair like the grass,
cut the grass, he will be exposed.

*

Had I gone to the doctors
of course they would've said I was crazy!
Can you imagine?—*Excuse me, Doctor Mangwana,*
I can feel a snake on my head. A heavy snake
unless I shave my head.
Ha! You would have spent your childhood
visiting me in the Maudsley.

*

So, I took the clippers, gave them to cousin Reginald and said,
take them, my husband won't understand, not being of our land.
Take them, help me.

*

Mum's orb of a 'fro lays on the red and gold carpet.
The clippers hum in Reginald's hand
long after he's pressed OFF. (*Off with her hair!*)

*

Mum's American sister—the one whose name
will not be said in our house, the betrayal too great
—enraged. Screaming into the mirror enraged.

*

Mum's bedroom—
half chapel, half boudoir.
It's a wig shop!
Wigs hang from the bed posts,
top corners of the mirror.
Tight curly wigs,
boob-length wigs,
red and black pom-poms. Jesus
unadorned by frame or glass,
tacked to the wall
above where Mum will later lay
her clean-shaven head to pray
till her knees and elbows are sore.

THE COW AND THE MOON

The cow is driven across the grate
to the metal milkers.

The cow has long, sad eyelashes.
Long, low and sad as feathered moons.

The cow can barely walk.
Her stick legs sprawl like tables laden

with three fatted calves,
a dozing husband.

The cow's udders are marigold gloves
blown out of all proportion.

Stuffed with Barbie's jeep, Duplo,
plastic fruit.

The cow is groaning.
Long, low and sad.

Groaning like a queen
arrowed to a sofa.

CAR SWEETNESS

Some long journeys back,
Mum would lay her hand
over Dad's on the gearstick,
their wedding rings glinting
like mouths not used to smiling.

BLOODLINES

It couldn't have been coke because
that would've made us high as kites. All those Es!

Must've been a can of orange or lemon fizzy.
Whatever it was, I opened it

all by myself in the backseat
and split my finger open.

Mum pivoted in the passenger, grabbed
and sucked my faucet finger.

She sucked it all the way down
the dual carriageway.

Dad didn't have any car tissues
What kind of man . . . ?

My finger, livid with embarrassment,
my blood salty, *surprisingly salty*

for a girl my age.

AND THEN THERE WAS THE TIME I GOT INTO A FIGHT

at three minutes to home-time cos they all said liar,
that weren't my dad come to pick me up for once,
a treat, right there, squinting in the sun—that one!
Holding his work-sack by the scruff—
top secret files inside: red, looming stickmen
by kids not looked after prop'ly. There! With the
light brown hair ('I wish you were still blonde, Dad.'
'Why?') See him, how trim, he runs every day,
even Christmas Day, yeah, come to pick me up,
his real, brown daughter. Him! On the other side
of the glass. I rattatat, jellyfish my mouth to it,
'Dad, wave to me!' 'Ain't your dad' 'Is! Look, Dad!'
Dad doesn't wave, he squints in the sun
(*Always frowning, Richard, face all lined up*)
Couldn't be they said. 'Liar,' George shrugged.

JAIL LETTER

All Saturday I sit viced between Mum's legs.
When it's dark and all my friends are inside she says,
Finished! like 'Ta-dah!' as if anything about this has been quick
or thrilling.

The corners of my eyes have been stitched into my hairline.
All the 'sheep's wool' they love to touch and say eww to at school
has been harvested into rows at the top of my head;
black crown or web.

'Mum, my scalp burns!'
'Ungrateful! Look at you, beautiful as Winnie Mandela!'
I don't know who this is,
but it doesn't sound like someone Ben Clark will fancy.

WIRE

Why's your sister's hair longer than yours?
How comes it's so long and soft and black
and yours isn't? It's way past her shoulders!
Can I touch it? I bet I can guess which one
your mum prefers styling in the morning.
When she was a baby, people would stop me
in the street to ask if her father was oriental!
So manageable, such a quiet curl.
Your sister's hair is proper mixed but yours
is afff-row! When your mum does those plait
things it looks like spiders *not* Winnie Mandela.
Do you have the same dad? Do you dream about
chopping hers off at night? I bet you do.
Don't lie! I can tell.

RED ROOF

She's 6, I'm 8.
Or she's 8, I'm 10.
Either way, she's small,
I'm massive. We sit
cross-legged in her red
and yellow playhouse.
The whole thing is fabric.
The numberless front door
velcro-locks. Either side,
two tiny windows; daytime
is a material we can't see out of.
I say, *Take your knickers off.*
Or we crawl in knickerless.
I don't remember seeing
a daisyed heap beside us.
Maybe we'd planned this.
Or I'd planned it solely.
Likely there was no plan,
just bored of playing church
or schools.
Now, I touch you then
you touch me.
No, I don't want to.
Why not? You have to.
She gags, *yours is hairy,*
monster. She dives

to tear up the door. I grab
her ankle. *It's normal!*
Mum checked
with the school nurse—who
curlicued a fingernail
into my elastic, peered inside
and catapulted them back,
disgusted.
Yours'll be a monster soon.
Won't! Just you.
True. Between her legs is
so light and clean. *Please.*
She tilts her head, weighs
this new power she has
over me, under this
red roof.
I touch hers quickly,
a brush so light
I could say I didn't
mean to, not really.
When she doesn't
scream, I take her
little hand, guide it
towards my ugly.

DANIELLE'S DAD

has magical pockets.
People come from all over the estate.
They pay and hurry away.
We watch from our bedroom window,
through bunkbed bars, we pretend we're in prison.
We ask Danielle, What sort of magic?
She says, Dunno.
Danielle is not very clever.
She thinks the Woolwich Ferry is the Titanic.
Look! She said as we drove around the roundabout,
The Titanic!
Even Mum pretended not to laugh.
When Danielle is playing over,
we can only play cheat-Scrabble
as she isn't very good at spellings or maths either.
We just write our names
then add our letters together.
Out of Rachel, Maria and Danielle,
I am the winner.
Sometimes, Danielle's dad reaches into his pocket
and yanks out a black Lab puppy called Bo.
Or a quadbike for JJ.
Or lacy pink curtains for their screaming mum.
But most often Danielle's dad yanks out fistfuls of coins.
The most coins I've ever seen in a real-life hand.
When we're playing out with Danielle, he'll say,

Oi, ghels, go get some iscream or sumfink.
We cheer, we shout, Thank you, Danielle's dad!
He doesn't even count it, just pours the thick gold
into our cupped hands till they bubble over.
We skip towards the ice cream man.
When we pay, we remember to cover our boobs
with our other hand. We don't take a lick
till we're back behind the garages.
As he kisses my earlobe before bed,
I tell Dad, Danielle's dad is richer than you.
Hmm, I bet he is, Dad says.

INSIDE

Mum's room
top drawer, knicker drawer
talcum, cotton, candle
stubs. There is, if you
swill the whitish surf, a black
notepad. A diary
isn't a diary till
you won't show anyone.

Inside that diary,
dead centre, you'll find
two lines of Mum's
almost aristocratic hand.
The ink cannot decide
if it is black or blue,
vow is underlined
Jehovah, if you save me I will—

DIVINE HEALING

Mum said Auntie B tried to palm her cancer off.
*High-up witches can do that—see a sickness coming
and deflect it.* Mum was driven to the seaside

to bathe at night, snow on the almost-sand,
then back to the corrugated church
where she was placed shivering before the Lord.

For seven days and seven nights, she lay in the rain
of the elders' ceaseless prayers. She'd forgotten the language
of her girlhood, but there, on the floor, remembered

three words and repeated, *Amin, Jesu Kristi.*
She rose only to use the bathroom, and the payphone once,
to call her agency: *I won't be available this week, I'm sorry.*

After the hunger had set deep
and the holy water had been sipped,
and the last candle had sputtered, pooled,

the police arrived
to carry Mum to the altar,
which was, she saw, as she got closer,

an operating table, basked in blue light.
I should say that in dreams/visions/parallel realities,
the police are angels. The tallest wielded a scalpel,

made an incision beneath her breast
and from that new smile dragged handfuls of teeth.
It took them all night. *But night there was so bright.*

And when Mum woke she was healed.
And Auntie B passed
the next year, leaving her two boys.

Is one not my own godson?
Mum straightened like a just queen,
B wouldn't have shed a tear if she'd gotten me in that box,

she saw it coming
and tried to derail that sickness of the breast to me.
Only God in his mercy—

Those angels, that night, they returned it to sender.
Stop crying!
It was B's sickness, her time.

NIGHT

is a short film you commissioned.
A red net curtain billowing in slow-mo.
At 1:22 a girl's face appears behind it.
Two brown hands—the camera's?—reach out,
find only fabric.

*

They're with us in this room.
Mum taught me how to feel them
on my back. How to plead The Blood,
thumb seven crosses between my blades,
in the centre of my forehead.
She didn't teach me how to lose them
on my way home from the shops.
If you can't find a tree,
walk three times around a parked car.
Don't look in the windows. Don't smoke
till you get home. They are attracted
to sadness.

*

I can still only tell if Mum is laughing
or crying by her breasts
—up-down for laughing, up-down
then into a heavy sway for crying.

*

Remember why you'd eat two dinners
then as many broken biscuits as it took to taste metal
on the roof of your mouth. You knew, somehow,
that to die was to be hungry.

*

Ha! You once thought heaven was a shack on a cloud,
Mary smiling serene, walking between the rows
of scythed corn-people
laid out on the bare floorboards.
You kept trying to get up
like the only live crab in a box.
Each night she squeezes your shoulder,
says, *Stay down.*
She has the voice of a social worker.

COMMUNION

after Deana Lawson

Behold the miracle of afro hair.
Blackness so complete
you could put your hand in,
never get it back. Recognise
the shark eyes of boredom,
the dial of two women
tending to every hair on your head
cussing a curve into a needle,
thick thread spooling,
the scissors are just there
but teeth are closer.
Ever sat for thirteen hours
in the same chair?
Scalp sliced so many times
you can't recall if you are girl
or railroad?
Ever not received what was meant to be
in the bag?—Softness, *Whappened?*
Ain't never seen no half-white hair like this!
Choose a new version of yourself
every 2–3 months. Be Russian, Hawaiian,
Virgin—at 8, 16,
22 inches. Go electric blue, blonde,
Faith Evans-auburn.
Enter the shabby palaces

named after the high priestesses;
En Vogue, Cleopatraz, Rihanna's;
promising next to nothing—
not an appointment, good service,
politeness, a mirror,
that you'll leave before dark;
to be left with half a head
so another customer can be squeezed in
for Ghana braids, you're kidding
if you think that a box of wings and chips
won't be eaten over your fresh weave,
leftover finger-grease used to smooth it.
Lord grant me serenity and deliver me
from the *Titanic* song by Celine Dion
on everlasting pull-up,
radio warbling atop wet towels,
but it's either Celine's heart going on and on
and on, or the cacophony of phone calls
about papers, Pampers, the price of meat.
Girl, you're the blackest you might ever be in here,
stop pulling away
from the crepe roll of her belly
over tightest jeans. Let it rise,
rest on your earlobe.
Dare to breathe regular on her hand;
Jackie, Marcia, Tat—omnipresent aunties

who won't flinch or say you breathe heavy.
When you are finally did,
you tip, she pockets it, saying,
dese little white pickney dem
always have money.

FUNERAL BROCHURE

Mum, when you're not here anymore
—in one hundred and fifty years or more!
('Amen', she'll say.) Well, what will we put on the front
of your funeral brochure?

Leave it blank, Mum says,
I hate pictures, and everyone there
should know that.

HOLIDAY ALBUM

She won't be in a single photograph!
She hides behind people and trees.
She won't come out till the flash has passed over.

She's absent from every family holiday.
Doesn't she care that we appear motherless
and heartless, grinning cheeese like we don't miss her.

We're motherless on an ocean liner,
crying in the restaurant the first time we try steak,
'the blood!' we're mouthing, *'the blood!'*

Motherless in the desert, on malnourished horseback.
Motherless against the ancient wall overlooking the bay
and shot at sunset on the last day.

THE OMEN

Dad said that when Mum first walked into class
she wore a question mark on her head.
A question mark? We laugh.

Yeah, it was sort of all brushed up on top of her head,
a plait thing sticking up, and she would pin one end down
like a question mark—on top of her head.

Ignore that man! Mum shouts from the kitchen.

DOLLS

INTERVIEW WITH B. TAPE II

Before he moved in it was peaceful.
All picnics, BBQs on blanket beaches,
long drives in pastel convertibles.

My Kenny had an army jeep,
which he got for an absolute steal from (sips tea) a neighbour.
He said when I rode in it,

I became even more perfect.
The contrast!—my angel face
against the camo.

Steve tried to threaten Kenny,
Kenny was just retaliating,
just protecting me—

Steve wore bright red swim shorts. Too bright.
Everything about those people is so . . .
you know?

Ken ripped those right off, my brave bull,
tossed them into the sea.
Steve was so black he never bruised, I mean

crime went up in the area! Tools all over the beach,
my Kenny having to keep a fork—a real fork
under his pillow, I said, Baby, leave it, forget him

but Kenny said it was the principle
and I giggled.
Kenny says my giggle is intoxicating.

He un-velcroed my ballgown,
right there on the beach, we—
(plays with pendant)

When I awoketh—that's the right word, isn't it—
Kenny was gone. My phone was back at the log cabin
along with my shoes. Otherwise I would've called or . . . (shrugs)

I don't like to talk about this—
OK, fine, he went looking
for Steve

Found him
walking home from the pool-bar he worked
Ken crimped him into the back of the jeep.

There was punching, kicking, spitting,
force—I mean, *allegedly* (rolls eyes,
stubs out cigarette)

But you know the worst thing?
(turns to Ken) Tell them, Baby,
tell them what you told me

—about the blood,
how it couldn't even well
in his eyes.

STEVE

was the black one   mum
must've bought him for us   we
wouldn't have asked for him
he was ugly   of course he fancied
princess barbie but her blue sparklies
were strictly for ken
we'd make them have s.e.x
surfboard chest against pert rock
breasts   slap and click of plastic
against plastic   we'd make
steve watch   dunk him in
the bath to cry
ken would beat steve up
for fun   till past bedtime
we'd wake to find steve sprawled
on the daisy carpet
butt-naked   the beatings got worse
slashes across rubber legs   face
coloured-in all red   the beatings
got more frequent   quickly before
school   before mum sees under
the table   it got so bad
even dad complained   his
lawnmower was jammed
on closer inspection
a tiny pair of shorts   charred
torso

BLACK PRINCESS! BLACK PRINCESS!

Before we go any further, we'll need a urine sample.
Glass of water, Madam? You'll be pleased to know
your parents have been fully vetted,
though that father is a cross to bear, isn't he?
Your mother is a breath of fresh air.
Though, shame about her listing her occupation as
'yoga teacher' not just 'teacher'.
We could have made something of that:
'Lecturer, Professor' etc.
You, Madam, went to a good school, didn't you?
Hollywood, I hear.
We're keen to avoid any awkward questions,
should they arise, about how a yogi single mother
could afford to send her daughter to a good school.
But, all verified, she's through!
Now, we must comb through your hair.
Just joking! We've attended training on that issue
but we will have to comb through every partner you've had—
sexual, oral, even one lingering look past platonic,
we'll need to know about it: first name, last name just here.
Don't be coy. If any name has 'slipped your mind',
then please be exact as possible with date, time, venue
and a full physical description; no one too difficult to find.
How many might we be expecting, Madam?
Do you know your blood type? When was your last period?
Smear? Chemical peel? Your doctors will be questioned,

nothing severe, just a gentle checking all is in order,
that your womb is suitably ermine-lined.
Your doctors will have to sign disclosures too
to protect you, themselves, and of course, The Family
—all being well, *your* family! Isn't that exciting?
A real pay-off some might say. Madam.

SELF-PORTRAIT WITH BABY

You don't even have a baby.
Haven't wanted one for a decade.
You did—not to hold
but hold over them; the boys you loved
and wanted to keep.
You wanted a good glue,
the most lasting,
to render them unable to forget or delete you.
Eww, those now-men parking up,
slamming doors, striding down your private path,
as they will next Friday, and the one after,
one after another, to your cottage door,
knocking on the stained-glass
because they're still barbaric.
You shudder, you must answer,
pull your cardigan together,
open your smart black door.
Don't let them in, don't let them all the way in
but they're close enough already,
up the step, on the welcome mat,
trainer toe-cap or arrowhead
of a smart shoe
over the skirting, on, touching
your scrubbed-up tiles.
You pick the baby up
from where she's been this whole time

—on the bench under the window.
How could you have missed her?
Curled cute as a prawn in her pink brushed cotton.
Blurry face, real hands, a hat
—as if she comes with a carrier!
A seat for a car you don't have and can't drive.
The baby is yours. You know it like hunger.
Hi, he says to his watch; ostentatious as ever
then reaches out, *I'll bring her back Monday.*
You're weak but lift the carrier
and hand her—your baby girl—over to him.
Or to him, or the other. They knock one after the other,
to collect and collect your babies,
which they say are also theirs; your babies together.
It's only fair, there were agreements
you can't break, you mustn't break
so you hand them over and over the threshold
and she goes, each time, she goes.

THANKSGIVING

As if by accident, I find my head
washed up window-side of his bed.
After all that fucking, look!
the sky's still pinned up.
His nose is longer with his eyes shut.
This whole time, I've been holding,
squeezing, wringing, folding,
bending, nodding, thank you, God,
for giving me someone who makes me hold
my breath. I will be so light
upon his life he won't realise
he's kept me.
I'll leave not a mark
on his pillow, papers,
knife, DVDs or wineglass.
What blessing
Only when he is sleeping
can I breathe out. So deep
my ribs come up like a ship.

OTHER WOMEN'S BABIES

Over Canada / or two hours of frozen waves I assume is Canada /
I'm surrounded by babies / so many babies / Mum, do you
remember X / the one you sometimes ask after / the one who knew
to bow for you / call you Ma outside that bookstore / Yes / him /
the one with the son / well he came to carry me over them all /
they were the eighth sea / they were that song that's supposed to be
reserved for God's love / you know the one that goes / *so high you
can't get over it, so wide* / Mum / you can't even fathom / so many
babies / all in a pile / all the babies ever born / or all the ones never
born / clamouring / wailing for me to choose / pick one / Now I
know why you said not to hold other women's babies / *carrying a
child not your own means wahala* / X folded me to his chest like / I
was the last deckchair of summer / He walked that walk men walk
when they're doing something noble / He set me down in a town
square / left me there / I was encircled by three witches / they
dripped oil on my forehead / tried to teach me a new and diabolical
language / James / our James / walked out of a municipal white
building / stood at my side / he'd been sent by you or higher / to
escort me out of that square / past the city limits /
his spirit was strong / it came in waves / the three witches did not /
or could not / stop us / leaving

ACKNOWLEDGEMENTS

Poems in this book have appeared in the following journals and magazines:

The London Magazine: 'Hotel Art, Barcelona' and 'The Clean' (October 2020)

The Poetry Review: 'Red Hoover', 'Orb', 'Referring to the House as the Whole Street', 'So Low', 'Mum's Snake', 'Car Sweetness', 'Jail Letter', 'Inside', 'Funeral Brochure', 'Holiday Album', and 'The Omen' (Summer 2020)

Aesthetica Magazine: 'Jail Letter' (Sept 2020)

Mal Journal: 'Red Roof' (published as 'Shamehouse'), 'Steve', 'Thanksgiving', and 'Other Women's Babies' (Oct 2019)

Granta: 'Communion' and 'Interview with B. Tape II' (July 2020)

Wasafiri Magazine: 'Self-Portrait with Baby' (March 2020)

I feel like I've been writing these acknowledgements since the beginning. Perhaps before the poems.

I would like to thank, first and foremost, my mother, for your protection and wisdom.

To my darling sister, there's so much we don't say to each other because we just know. I hope that you know all that I am saying to you here.

To my father, for being a kind and gentle man.

To my brother. The blessing.

To Antosh Wojcik, thank you for giving me the love and space to write this book.

To my girl, Elaine Castillo. I was struck by you from the first. How lucky am I to have met you?—to have a friend who is as fierce in life as she is on the page. I'm wary of regarding people as inspirational, but you are. Your love is a lesson.

To Fabien, for the space you give Elaine and me to be girls and women and writers and sisters all in one video call that lasts the whole afternoon. The things I've realised at your table, in London or California, are dear.

My dearest Tiffany, for growing up with me.

I would like to thank the organisations who have supported me, the incredible people who make them up, and the kin I have come to know through them.

From the beginning, that first poetry workshop at The Albany, in Deptford, with Jean 'Binta' Breeze. Thank you to Apples and Snakes, and particularly to Daisy Dockrill, who called my work beautiful when it most certainly was not. Dais, look what you made happen by telling me that lovely lie.

To Jacob Sam-La Rose, thank you for encouraging and championing my work from the first. For making it so I could not only write poems but live on and by them.

To Caroline Bird, I would not be the poet I am without you. This book would not exist (another might but it would be crap). Working with you accelerated everything.

To Jack Underwood, for all you taught me about poetry in the pub.

To Raymond Antrobus for creating that space. For your 'check ins'.

To Bea Colley, for being a bright and brilliant woman who uplifts others.

To my smart and kind agent, Emma Paterson at Aitken Alexander.

To the incredible team at Tin House. I am so glad to have a US home with you. To Elizabeth DeMeo for your enthusiasm for my book, for all your meticulously hard work. My utmost thanks to the whole team: Craig Popelars, Nanci McCloskey, Becky Kraemer, Alyssa Ogi, Jakob Vala, Yashwina Canter, Lanesha Reagan, and to Louisa Wells for your art, for this stunning cover, which I fell in love with instantly!

To my UK team at Picador: Kishani Widyaratna, Alice Dewing, Don Paterson and Ami Smithson.

To all my sisters in Octavia.

To Amaal Said for being the artist and friend I trust enough to take my photograph.

To Arts Council England for making it possible for me to take the time this book needed. It made such a difference.

To the Southbank Centre, The Poetry School, Spread the Word, and The Arvon Foundation.

To Roger Robinson, Kathryn Maris, Bernardine Evaristo, Nick Makoha, Peter Kahn, Mona Arshi, Joanna Brown, Yomi Sode, Edward Doegar, Clare Pollard and Wayne Holloway-Smith, for all the ways you have each been encouraging of my work.

Lastly, I would like to thank all the people who invite me to be part of your projects or events, who come to my readings and workshops. The girl in me who is still writing in a corner of her room is particularly grateful.